PAUL McCARTNEY

THE ILLUSTRATED
PAUL McCARTNEY

GEOFFREY GIULIANO
BRENDA GIULIANO

CHARTWELL
BOOKS, INC.

Published by
CHARTWELL BOOKS, INC.
A Division of **BOOK SALES, INC**
110 Enterprise Avenue
Secaucus, New Jersey 07094

Produced by Sunburst Books,
Deacon House, 65 Old Church Street, London SW3 5BS.

ISBN 1 55521 873 3

Printed and bound in Hong Kong

CONTENTS

DEDICATION

With love to Sesa, Devin, Avalon, and India, our Fab Four.

A CHARMED LIFE

"rs. James Paul McCartney." Isn't that what all eleven-year-old girls in 1964 wanted to grow up to be? The privileged wife of the cute Beatle. Of course, each of the Beatles had a profound effect on my life. They colored my initial outlook on the world and later encouraged me to see society as questionable and challenging authority whenever and wherever it fell short.

Paul McCartney was always extremely sensitive, but nonetheless flirty and fun. He and his musical colleagues heralded ideals of love and peace I could easily identify with and paved the way for a life of activism in the realm of animal rights and innate spirituality I hold dear to this day. When he married Linda in 1969, I suppose it was a blow to all of us true female fans, but she too, was ultimately a positive influence for me. They were both strict vegetarians and loving parents that encouraged free thinking in their children and maintained a very close knit, open, family atmosphere.

Paul too, generally said what he thought. When asked tough questions by the media like, "Have you taken LSD?" or "Do you smoke marijuana?", it was such a relief to hear somebody finally shoot from the hip and not be afraid to talk a little truth, no matter what the consequences. Pre-Fab Four, back in the dusty Fifties, many families only seemed close., not from any meaningful interaction with one another, but inevitably stood apart acting out a very strained, forced respect. Upon reflection, it seemed an especially mean time when any open, honest communication was generally looked down upon. The Beatles helped to change all that as well.

McCartney was open. Sure, he did some drugs way back when and perhaps slept with a few too many dolly birds, but I never felt I had to

actually be like him. I just wanted to be open and honest with myself and everyone around me.

Now that I'm grown and have children of my own I appreciate Paul and Linda's ongoing support for animal rights, protection of the rain forests, the choking ozone and their up front stand on ethical vegetarianism. Amazingly, the phenomenal success the McCartneys still enjoy keeps them out there and they never miss a chance to try and gently educate the public – just as The Beatles were doing throughout the Sixties. Not only did they help wake up an entire generation, but they've kept us on our toes, oh, these many years.

Paul, ironically, inspired me to defy my parents for the first time. My cousin Cathy and I thought we'd somehow be drawn closer to our four romantic heroes if we had Beatle haircuts and so went out and had our waist length hair cut to Beatle form. When my parents saw me for the first time all they could say was, "You know you're not allowed to cut your hair!"

"Well, I wanted to!" I shot back defiantly. That was my very first stab at independence, and it felt great. Thanks, Paul.

Brenda Giuliano
"Skyfield"
Western New York
1993

CHAPTER ONE

DISTANT SHORES/CHILDHOOD

McCartney waves to the ever-present paparazzi on one of the Beatles' early European tours.

Nobody in Paul McCartney's family can remember a time when they didn't reside in Liverpool. For well over a hundred years now the clannish, closeknit McCartneys have called England's largest seaport home.

McCartney's father, James, one of nine children, was born July 7, 1902, to tobacco cutter Joseph, and mother Florence Clegg, at 8 Fishguard Street, Everton, one of Liverpool's roughest neighborhoods. Educated peripherally at nearby Steer Street School, Jim was partial to music and taught himself piano, after a fashion, on an old upright.

"My dad was actually a pretty fair pianist, you know," McCartney commented recently. "He played by ear, his left one! Actually, he was deaf in one ear."

A gregarious, young man-about-town, Jim met his future wife, pretty Mary Patricia Mohin after the start of the Second World War at the McCartney family home at 11 Scargreen Avenue, West Derby. Mary, a nurse at nearby Walton Hospital on Rice Lane, was staying temporarily with Jim's newlywed sister Jin and her husband, Harry Harris, and had stopped by to visit the McCartneys that evening after work. Coincidentally, that same night the Third Reich showered Liverpool's busy harbor with bombs, forcing Jim and Mary to spend the night huddled together downstairs.

Born on September 29, 1909, at 2 Third Avenue, Fazakerly, Liverpool, Mary was one of four children.

They officially tied the knot on April 15, 1941, in a full church wedding at St. Swithin's Roman Catholic Church, Gill Moss, in Liverpool. Thereafter they took furnished rooms on Sunburys Road, Anfield. Not long afterwards, work at the Cotton Exchange was suspended. Unfit for military service due to his advancing age (thirty-nine) and rup-

Paul cops a kiss from a friendly fan following a late-night remix for the *White* album.

Paul McCartney is an extremely proficient musician, having mastered several instruments including bass, guitar, clarinet, trumpet and, as witnessed here, drums.

tured eardrum, McCartney found work at Napier's aircraft factory as a center lathe turner, helping to manufacture fighter planes. He also worked as a firefighter.

Their first child, James Paul, was born on June 18, 1942, in a private ward in Walton Hospital. As Mary had been an employee of long standing, the head nurse waived the normal visiting hours and allowed the senior McCartney to visit mother and son whenever he wished. "He looked awful, I couldn't get over it," Mr. McCartney recalled. "When I got home I cried, the first time for years and years... But the next day he looked more human. And every day after that he got better and better. He turned out a lovely baby in the end."

Intent on seeing her little family steadily move up in the world, by 1949 Mary had wangled yet another new home from the council, this one a large, reasonably well-equipped row house at 12 Ardwick Road on the outer reaches of Speke. Shortly after moving in, the little McCartney lads almost lost their lives by falling into a nearby rain-filled lime pit their father had repeatedly warned them against, made even more deadly by the fact that neither of the brothers had yet learned how to swim. After much hysterical thrashing about, Mike was finally able to grab onto an old tree limb, thus holding them both aloft until a neighbor heard their pitiful pleas for help and came to the rescue.

Their first school was Stockton Wood Road Infants' School.

Consistently popular with both his masters and schoolmates, Paul was voted "head boy" several times.

Characteristically eager to please those he perceived to be in positions of authority, inwardly McCartney harbored very mixed feelings about his life at school. "Homework was a right drag," he later confessed in Hunter Davies' *The Beatles: The Authorized Biography*.

Later the footloose McCartney family moved house again. This time home was a neat and airy row house at 20 Forthlin Row, in Allerton. Tragically, on October 31, 1956, Mary McCartney died suddenly after an operation for breast cancer at Liverpool's Northern Hospital. Paul was only fourteen, Mike was twelve.

The week of the funeral Paul and Mike went to stay with their Auntie Jin, their father having no wish for them to see him so badly broken up. Mary was finally laid to rest on November 3, 1956, at Yew Tree Cemetery, on Finch Lane, Huyton.

Not surprisingly, after Mary died life on Forthlin Row was far different for the McCartneys. Jim, of course, was now forced to be both breadwinner and full-time housekeeper. Although his sisters, Mill and Jin, helped out when and where they could, it was still a terrible strain on the fifty-three-year-old salesman.

As children neither of the boys really showed any special interest in music. Their father did sign them up for piano lessons as youngsters but made the mistake of starting them in the summer when all their

The famous front gates to Strawberry Fields Children's Home in suburban Liverpool

Opposite: **Paul McCartney dragging on a long cigarette and wearing a Mexican-style moustache, popular in the Sixties.**

Paul McCartney's boyhood home in Liverpool

little mates were buzzing around outside, wanting them to come out to play. After about two or three lessons, getting them to practice became a high-stress situation and so, reluctantly, Jim allowed them to quit. Later he insisted Paul try out for a spot in the Liverpool Cathedral Choir but he resisted and apparently deliberately cracked his voice at the audition. Eventually though, Paul did sing in the St. Chad's Choir off Penny Lane for a time but soon tired of the choirmaster's overly regimented approach and dropped out.

His first instrument, a low budget acoustic, soon became the overriding force in his life. "It's funny, but everyone remembers their first string box," he recalls. "Mine was a Zenith. I'd no idea where it was going to lead at the time ... I started bashing away and pretty soon had the basic chords well and truly learned. Then I got a bit more ambitious and bought a solid Rosati (a "Lucky Seven"). It only had two strings and when I played it, it didn't produce a very melodic sound. But I kept the volume right down and it seemed okay to me."

Along with McCartney's interest in the guitar came a growing awareness of rock'n'roll. Before long it wasn't just the music that had captured his imagination but the whole freewheeling, rock lifestyle as well. A fellow classmate at the Institute, Ian James, also took up the guitar, and soon the two were cycling around Liverpool with their instruments strapped to their backs, looking for places to play. Much to Jim McCartney's dismay Paul had even taken to wearing the sort of clothes a guitar-picking teddy boy might choose. With his long, slicked-back hair, piled high above his forehead, narrow drainpipe trousers, and white, sparkly sportscoat, his perpetually innocent, choirboy face seemed incongruous. At fourteen he was far from being a tough Liverpool teddy boy, but he was also ivy leagues away from being the proper English schoolboy his father would have preferred.

Hopping on board the bus for the dreamy, half-hour morning ride to school, McCartney soon made friends with the driver's son, George Harrison, who, like McCartney, was smitten with the guitar. The two soon started hanging out together after school and inevitably began the thankless job of teaching themselves the new chords necessary to carry forward their boyish fantasies of one day playing in a big group.

Those fantasies would soon move a major step closer to reality.

Overleaf: **Being photographed with people he didn't know was one of McCartney's biggest gripes during the heyday of Beatlemania. Here, both John and Paul sit through yet another boring encounter.**

Beatles manager Brian Epstein and Paul together at EMI, 1966. Although he respected Epstein's theatrical flair, McCartney was unimpressed by his limited business acumen.

CHAPTER TWO

SKY HIGH/THE TEEN YEARS

Paul and Jane, the romantic "perfect couple" whose much-publicized relationship hid a lot of deeply private pain

Opposite: Macca, circa 1967

Paul McCartney's fortuitous first meeting with John Lennon officially took place on July 6, 1957, at a garden fete at St. Peter's Parish Church in Woolton.

That year, as a concession to the basically church-shy teenage youth of Woolton, following a blessing by the Reverend Maurice Pryce-Jones, a local group of lads known as the Quarry Men were slated to appear. Performing mostly covers of well-known rock and skiffle tunes, the five young men jived their way through a rapid-fire repertoire of numbers ranging from *Maggie May*, to *Railroad Bill* and *Cumberland Gap*.

In those days the Quarry Men were Colin Hanton on drums, Rod Davis, banjo, Len Gary, bass, Eric Griffiths, guitar, Pete Shotton, washboard, and of course John Lennon, guitar and lead vocal. Mixed into the happily swaying crowd was Paul McCartney who'd come along for the day at the suggestion of Ivan Vaughan, a mutual friend of John and Paul.

After the Quarry Men's swinging first set, Ivan led Paul across the road to the band's impromptu dressing room in St. Peter's Church Hall. "This is John," Vaughan ventured upon entering the large, sweltering room. "Hi," replied Lennon. "This is Paul." A rather ordinary beginning perhaps, but within minutes things heated up when it was discovered that McCartney not only played a pretty mean left-handed guitar, but wonder of wonders, could actually correctly tune one as well. "Neither John nor Eric Griffiths had learned how to do that yet," recalls longtime Beatle crony Pete Shotton, "Whenever their guitars went out of tune, they'd been taking them round and paying a fellow in King's Drive to do it."

McCartney further wowed the often standoffish Lennon by jotting

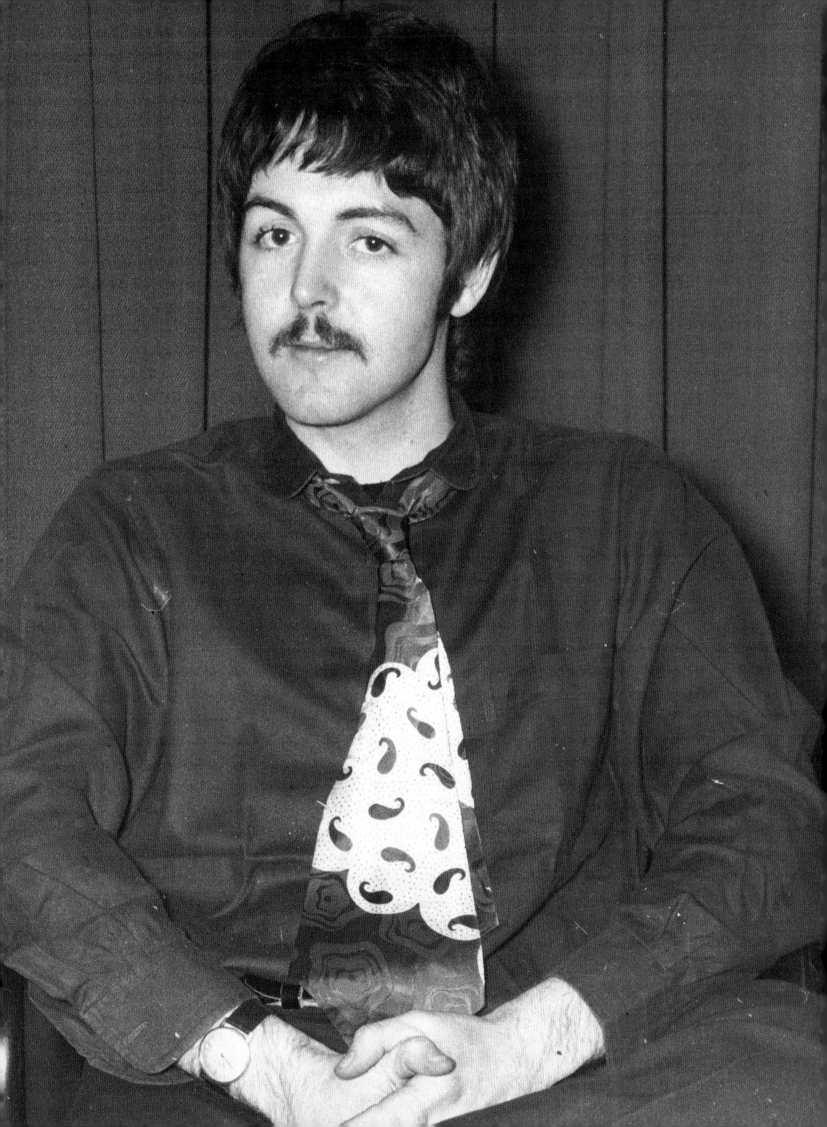

Signing for a fan, 1967

down the somewhat convoluted lyrics to singer Eddie Cochran's classic, *Twenty Flight Rock*, as well as Gene Vincent's crazy *Be-Bop-A-Lula*. He recounts what happened next, "I met them in the church hall. We talked and then I picked up a guitar lying there and started to play *Twenty Flight Rock*. I suppose I was showing off a bit. I knew all the words and they didn't. That was big currency. Then I went through all the stuff I knew. John seemed quite impressed. There was nearly two years between us, so he was a big man in my eyes."

Two weeks later, while cycling along Menlove Avenue in Woolton, McCartney ran into Shotton who offhandedly announced that John had been talking about him and wondered if he would like to join the band. Delicately balancing against the curb on his bike, McCartney reflected for a moment or two and then replied simply, "Okay then. See you," before shoving off back across the golf course to the willowy wilds of Allerton. McCartney was naturally pretty excited, inwardly anyway. Externally though he was typically nonchalant, hardly mentioning a word to anyone at home that night about his big break.

McCartney's first gig with the Quarry Men took place on October 18, 1957, at the New Clubmoor Club in Liverpool's Broadway. Resplendent as they were in their long, dark, string ties, black trousers, white shirts, and coffee-coloured sportscoats, their perfor-

Opposite: **The Fab Four as we remember them best**

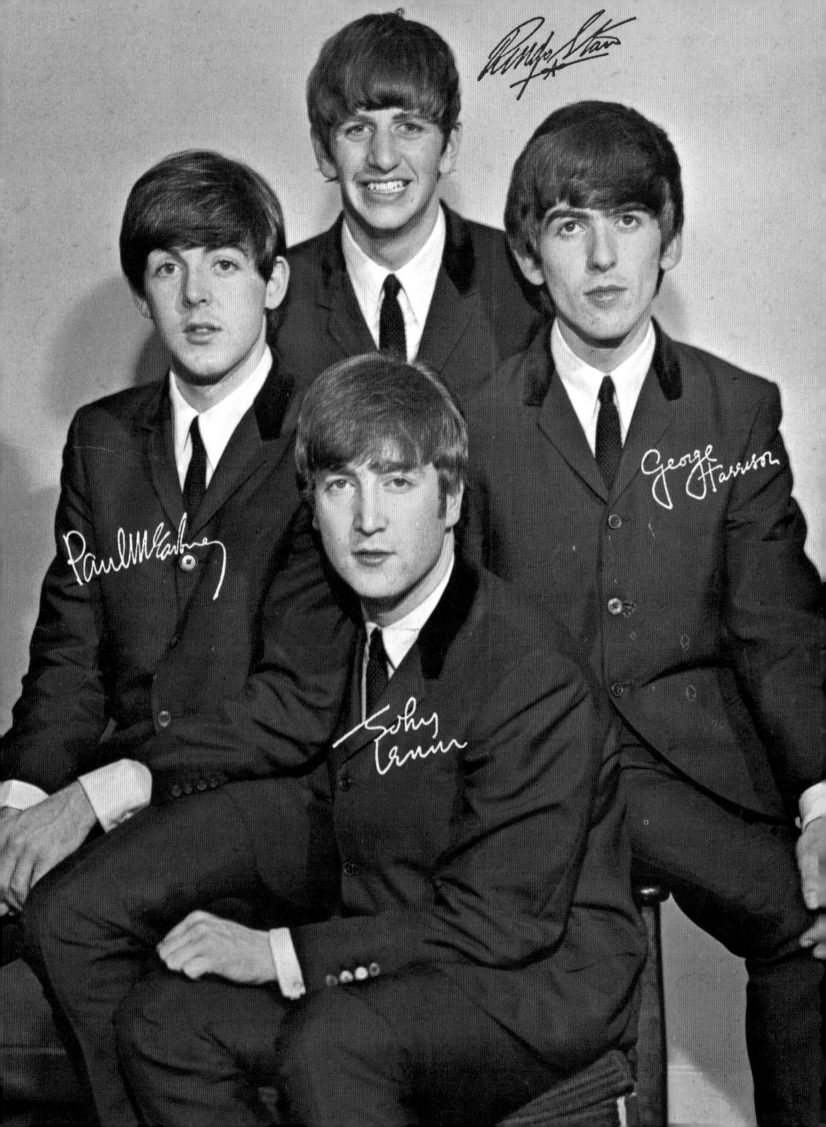

mance was apparently not up to the mark. "Good & Bad" was the cryptic assessment written on the band's visiting card by dance promoter Charlie McBain following McCartney's sorry attempt at lead guitar. "He really cocked up on this lone song," Lennon later recalled. "It was Arthur Smith's *Guitar Boogie*, a tune we all especially liked. When it came time for the big solo Paul lost his bottle and was all thumbs. The rest of the evening actually went down pretty smooth. We all had a good laugh about it afterwards, everyone, that is, except Paul."

During the first three years of their relationship John and Paul wrote literally dozens of songs together. Unfortunately, many of them were inadvertently lost when Paul's girlfriend, Jane Asher, tossed out an

In Scotland with Jane Asher

original notebook containing some of the first-ever Lennon/McCartney compositions while she was clearing out a cupboard in McCartney's St. John's Wood home. Included among the early tunes that have been preserved are *Catswalk, Hello Little Girl, Hot as Sun, Just Fun, Keep Looking That Way, Like Dreamers Do, Looking Glass, Love Me Do, That's My Woman, The One After 909, Thinking of Linking!, Too Bad About Sorrows, Winston's Walk,* and *Years Roll Along,* to name

Arriving at Heathrow with young Julian Lennon in tow

Paul, Jane and Martha, McCartney's heralded sheepdog

Paul

Opposite: The Beatles in the woods outside London during the filming of their second feature, *Help.*

Right: McCartney on tour here with Jane Asher

Below: Producing a session with The Black Dyke Mills Band, 1968

A little outdoor recording on a lovely summer day

Above: Running a gauntlet of fans and well-wishers following the McCartneys' wedding

Opposite: **Catching a few rays in LA in the mid-Seventies**

McCartney hitting the skins on location during the filming of *Magical Mystery Tour.* **Owing to the costume he is wearing, the wide-spread rumor that Paul was indeed the Walrus can now be confirmed. Removing the heavy latex head for a bit of fresh air must have provided welcome relief.**

just a few.

During this time Paul was still quite friendly with George Harrison, who despite his tender years impressed McCartney with his strong musical presence and stirring guitar licks, a commodity very much missing from the often musically adhoc Quarry Men.

Oscillating between the potential harm admitting Harrison to the group might have on Lennon's carefully crafted, tough guy, teddy boy image, and the obvious benefits of bringing on board a lad of such superior musicianship, Lennon finally relented when on February 6, 1958, he agreed to hear what George could do. "I listened to him play," Lennon recalled, "and I said, 'Play "raunchy,"' or whatever the old story is, and I let him in ... That was three of us then. The rest of the group was thrown out gradually ... We went for the strongest format, and for equals."

Being a Quarry Man, however, was not all adolescent merriment. Perpetually short of money and places to play, several times the group almost folded.

Casting off the extraneous Quarry Men along the way, the group

was now down to the three hard-core members – John, Paul, and George. Any sort of reasonable drummer, as usual, was almost impossible to find, or to keep. Altogether Lennon's schoolboy group played only about twenty-five official gigs over a three-year period, more for the experience than anything else. Still, the nucleus of what would later become the Beatles was now firmly fixed.

By the fall of 1959 John had finally dropped the name Quarry Men for the more celestial-sounding Moondogs, and then, Johnny and the Moondogs. It was during an on-stage audition for British television personality Carroll Levis (probably on October 18) that the boys first used the name. And although they made it into the finals (appearing for two successive auditions at the Liverpool Empire and Hippodrome theatres in Manchester), they were not ultimately chosen to appear on Levis's show.

Ever intent upon cultivating their blossoming image, the group tried on several new names over the following year, including the Beatals, the Silver Beats, the Silver Beetles, the Silver Beatles, and by August of 1960, the Beatles. Earlier that year, in January, Lennon invited his art school chum, Stuart Fergusson Victor Sutcliffe or simple "Stu" to join the band. Although a brilliant painter and designer, Sutcliffe made no pretense about being any sort of musician and was therefore obliged to pick up the bass as he went along, a learning experience that certainly didn't ingratiate him to the perfectionistic McCartney.

Paul outside his London home

By April 1960 things were finally beginning to perk up for the band. At this point still the Silver Beatles, the boys snagged a solid two weeks' work backing balladeer Johnny Gentle on a ballroom tour of Scotland. Encouraged by what for them was at least a taste of real work, they came home feeling like genuine musicians, even if their pockets were still basically just as empty as ever. "Someone actually asked me for my autograph," Paul wrote home to his dad from Inverness. "I signed for them too, three times!"

"From that day onwards," Jim McCartney later remarked, "things were never really quite the same."

Contrary to popular belief, the Beatles' initial trek to Germany came about more as a result of a lack of alternatives than of any great success in England. Thinking they had been booked at Hamburg's popular Kaiserkeller through small-time Liverpool promoter Allan Williams, they later discovered they were actually slated to appear as the new house band at the Indra, a seedy, low-life, former strip club at 34 Grosse Freiheit. Just prior to setting off, Paul McCartney rang up local drummer Pete Best on the spur of the moment and invited him to join the group as a quick fix to the Beatles' ongoing percussion problems.

The original *Magical Mystery Tour* bus

Opposite: **Happy family**

Paul and Linda stop by for a quick blessing from the local vicar in St. John's Wood after their wedding, March 12, 1969.

There was, however, still one major stumbling block to be overcome before the five eager young men could pile into Williams' battered green Mini-van and make for Germany: Jim McCartney. Aware that his no-nonsense dad would never allow such an apparently foolhardy venture without a great deal of convincing, Paul, ever the politician, cleverly recruited the assistance of his brother. After Paul's stirring fifteen-minute speech on how his phenomenal fifteen-pounds-a-week salary would enable him to buy his beloved younger brother just about anything his heart desired, Mike was only too happy to go a couple of rounds with the old man on Paul's behalf.

When the time came to actually make his pitch, however, Mike's impassioned pleas fell on deaf ears. Puffing thoughtfully on his ever-present pipe, Jim listened patiently before quietly lowering the boom. "I'm sorry, son, but the answer is no. The whole thing is just too uncertain."

"But he's got weeks of school holiday left," Mike went on, "and he'll be making fantastic money. I wish I had the chance to travel like that.

You're always going on about how broadening it is for a man to travel."

"That may be," Jim continued, "but we haven't even had the results of Paul's A Levels yet. If he were smart he'd be more concerned about that than gallivanting off with some beat group."

Despite Mike's best efforts, his father remained stubbornly unmoved and so Allan Williams went on to paint a picture of the lovely Germanic scenery, good steady wages, and a chance for his son to experience new, meaningful horizons. In other words, he laid it on thick.

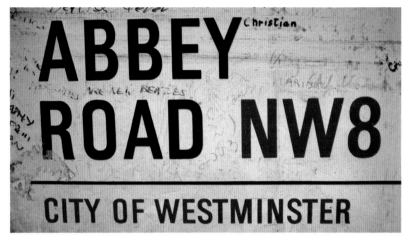

One of the world's most famous streets

The reality, however, was rather grim. When the boys first arrived they were put up not in the comfortable, homey, guest houses they had been promised back home, but rather three dank, seamy rooms with bunk beds behind the movie screen of the Bambi Cinema at 33 Paul-Roosen Strasse. Stuck away in their revolting, dilapidated digs, the boys looked around in utter disbelief.

"What a fucking shit hole," Lennon finally blurted out, suddenly pacing the almost pitch-black room like a wounded animal.

"Is this supposed to be a joke?" Paul asked no one and everyone. "Where's the bloody toilet?"

"We're living in it," George shot back sardonically.

"Not for fucking long I hope," countered Pete. "Allan should have seen to this lot."

"I'm knackered lads," said Lennon, finally throwing himself into one of the top bunks. "Welcome to the wonderful world of show business. Let's get some sleep."

Unfortunately, he spoke a moment too soon. Bone-tired from the gruelling trip, disoriented and hungry, the boys were all just about to settle down for a much-needed rest when a big, burly bouncer from the club ambled in and announced that the band was expected on stage at the Indra within the hour. Groaning and cursing together almost in unison, they had no alternative but silently to gather up their ragged gear and do as they were told. All things considered, their first taste of the continent left a lot to be desired.

The Beatles' first stint in Hamburg ended on November 21, 1960, when George Harrison was deported by immigration officials for working in a night club under the age of eighteen.

Brian Epstein's Liverpool grave

Within days Paul had reluctantly landed a "proper" job as a delivery boy for something called Speedy Prompt Delivery Service, in Liverpool.

CHAPTER THREE

TALL TALES / BEATLEMANIA

Above: **Partying in New Orleans during Wings' famous Wings Over America Tour of 1976.**

Opposite: **Little drummer boy, Paul, 1971**

One of the quiet turning points for the Beatles was their accidental meeting, in 1960, with future Cavern Club compere, Bob Wooler.

At this point, Stu was still in Hamburg, having fallen in love with arty young photographer Astrid Kirchherr, which quite inconveniently left open his position on bass. To fill the gap a young chemistry student, Chas Newby, was quickly ushered in, first playing with the group on December 17 at the Casbah Club, a smokey teenage dance cellar run by Pete Best's fun-loving mother, Mona.

Almost immediately the Beatles became the hottest thing going. Soon, however, Newby left the group to continue his studies, shifting his duties on bass to Paul.

Hand in hand with the Beatles' rapidly rising popularity began the manic adulation which was later to become the true hallmark of Beatlemania.

One of McCartney's "fave raves" during this period was Iris Caldwell, the pretty blonde sister of fabled Liverpool rocker Rory Storm. The romance lasted about a year and six months, during which time they both all but stopped seeing other people.

Eventually, in 1964, Iris married singer Shane Fenton (later to become seventies glitter king, Alvin Stardust), and accompanied him out on the road as part of his stage show. During her days with Paul however, there was never anyone else, at least for her. McCartney, she suspects, may have still occasionally sowed a few wild oats.

The Beatles' second trip to Hamburg commenced on Friday, March 24, 1961, with the boys loading their tatty gear into the baggage car of a Liverpool train and then scrambling for a seat together in second

Lennon in his adopted home of New York
City shortly before his death

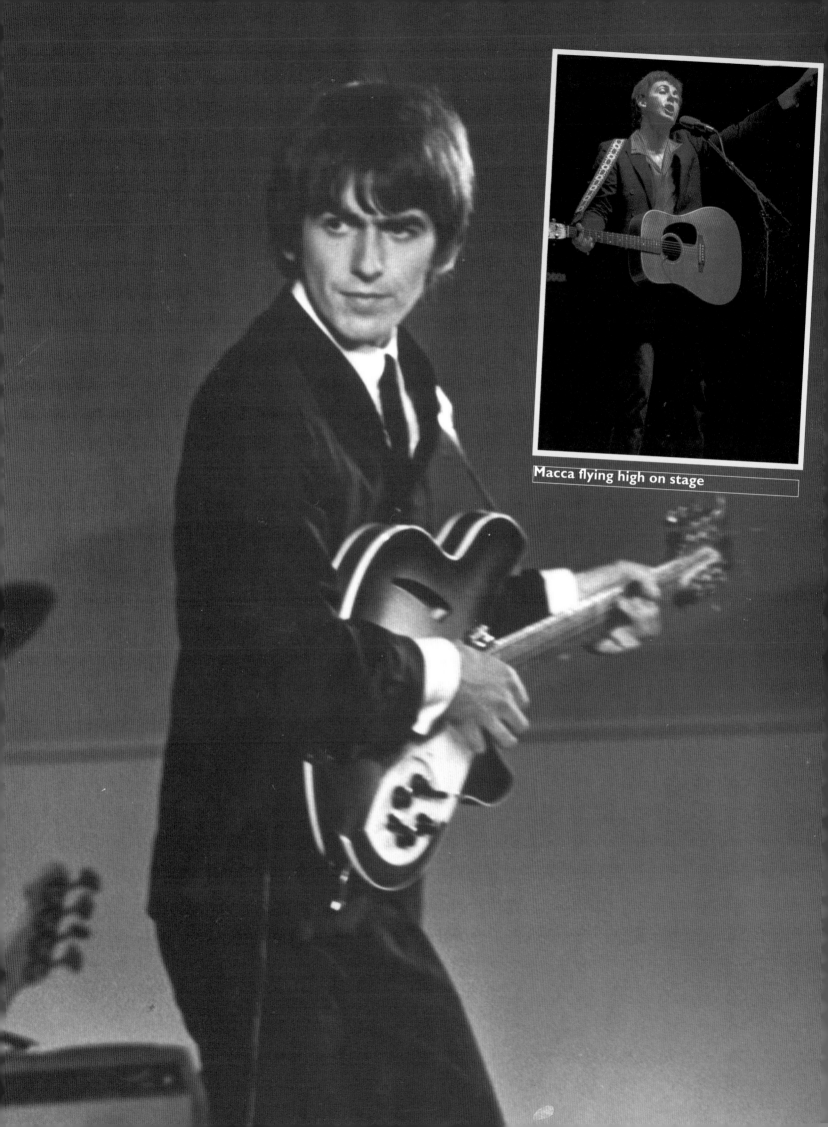

Macca flying high on stage

Above: **Performing *Hey Jude* on the David Frost Show, 1968**

Right: **Hiding out in Highlands, 1969**

Previous page: **Barnstorming America at the heady heights of Beatlemania**

class. Arriving exhausted, three days later, they stumbled into a taxi for the ten-minute-plus ride to their new, somewhat improved digs, supplied courtesy of promoter Peter Eckhorn, four shaky flights above their latest venue, the Top Ten Club.

Their salary was a duly modest thirty-five Deutsche Marks per bobbing Beatle. Not a fortune by any means, but mixed in with the many attractive perks the boys enjoyed on the Reeperbahn, it was enough to scrape by. The contract, negotiated over Mona Best's telephone by the band, demanded basically the same gruelling schedule as their earlier trek. They would perform nightly from 7.00 p.m. until 2.00 a.m., Monday through Friday. Weekends, they played an hour later, switching off their ragged amps at 3.00 a.m. Every hour on the hour they were entitled to a fifteen-minute break, plus all the free beer and booze they could manage to guzzle.

By this time, Stu had quite rightly decided to leave the band permanently in order to concentrate on his art work, not to mention his smoldering affair with Astrid. Occasionally, however, he would still sit

Above left: **The McCartneys arrive home at 7 Cavendish Avenue, St. John's Wood, London, on their wedding day.**

Above right: **Paul, Linda and little Heather arriving at Heathrow, September 1976**

in with the lads, and sometimes even with other visiting Liverpool groups as well. Music was definitely still very important to Sutcliffe but it was his love and respect for John Lennon that compelled him to stay close. That notion, apparently, was one of the few things he and Paul McCartney had in common.

The unquestioned highlight of this particular visit to Hamburg had to be the Beatles' first professionally produced recording session, held, disappointingly, onstage at an infants' school somewhere in Hamburg's lookalike suburbs.

For their work on the session the Beatles received a token three hundred Deutsche Marks each, as a one-time fee, thereby surrendering any further rights or royalties to the project. Ironically, a single pulled from the session, *My Bonnie*, backed by a hardrocking Lennon rendition of *The Saints*, eventually went on to sell an estimated 100,000 copies after reaching number five on the West German hit parade early that fall. The boys weren't even properly credited on the label of the disc, billed only as The Beat Brothers, Beatles apparently

Denny Laine: a stellar talent never fully realized
due to a series of largely undeserved,but brutal,
bad breaks

Weaving that old McCartney magic on stage in the seventies

Above right: **Filming the video for McCartney's** *Take it away* **off the brilliant** *Tug of War* **album**

Above top: **Denny Laine and a Wings roadie confer over a technical matter.**

Above: **Joe English late of Paul McCartney and Wings, 1977**

sounding a bit too close to the German schoolboy expression for the male organ, "peedle." It wouldn't be the last time they were referred to in that regard either.

The Beatles' second trip to Hamburg ended on July 2, 1961, after their twice-extended contract with Peter Eckhorn finally came to an end. Nine days later, Paul McCartney was comfortably back home with his father and brother enthusiastically plotting for the future.

Now securely under the tutelage of Brian Epstein, the Beatles cut a significantly more professional image due in large part to their new manager's well-honed sense of style and passion for the theatrical. Henceforth, they were strictly forbidden to swear, chew gum, or, God forbid, drink or eat on stage, prohibitions particularly irksome to the naturally rebellious Lennon. McCartney on the other hand, ever the promoter, clearly saw the wisdom of it all and actively encouraged the group to toe the line. "At least until we get what we want," he would mutter under his breath to John.

It was these new improved Beatles who jetted off to Hamburg on April 10, 1962, to begin their third stint on the Reeperbahn. This time,

Wings, mach one, circa 1973

thanks to Epstein's fastidious advance planning and skillful PR, they would play the Star Club, then one of Hamburg's most upmarket, high-paying venues. Just as they were about to leave for Speke Airport, however, an urgent telegram was received from Astrid. Cut down at the Kirchherr's home in Altona by the final one of many blinding attacks, Stu was rushed by ambulance to the hospital, unconscious and only barely alive. He never made it, dying enroute, cradled in Astrid's arms.

The devastating news hit the Beatles like a bomb. John burst into hysterical laughter, unable to stop. George became predictably quiet, while Paul, despite his long record of run-ins with the former Beatle, appeared genuinely shocked and upset. So did Pete. That same day, Paul, Pete, and John flew on to Germany, meeting Astrid at the airport for a somber, tearful reunion. George, Brian, and Millie Sutcliffe, meanwhile, arrived the next afternoon, joining Astrid and the other three for an unusually demonstrative, emotionally charged encounter in the arrivals lounge. Grasping for something comforting to say to Mrs. Sutcliffe, Paul reportedly told the grieving fifty-four-year-old woman that within six months of his mother's passing, most of the deepest hurt had disappeared. Millie smiled weakly. "That's because you are young," she replied softly through her tears. "It's different when you're my age, Paul."

Within days of the Beatles' solemn arrival in Germany, Lennon and McCartney, still enthusiastically pursuing their songwriting partnership, had penned a tune then called *Love, Love Me Do*. Both knew it was a good song, "a keeper," as Lennon put it, and he went right to work creating a catchy harmonica riff for the intro. The duo was beginning to take its composing duties a little more seriously than before, soon amassing a considerable portfolio of well-structured, upbeat material.

To everyone's complete surprise and delight, an urgent telegram was received from Brian Epstein in London on May 9, 1962, after he had finally secured a provisional recording contract for the group with Parlophone, a small subsidiary of the vast EMI empire: "CONGRATU-LATIONS BOYS. EMI REQUEST RECORDING SESSION. PLEASE REHEARSE NEW MATERIAL."

The four young men were on top of the world. This was it – the big break they had all been waiting for. And Eppy had made it happen.

Party Time!

"I told ya he was alright," said Lennon, gleefully jostling Paul as they read and then re-read the stiff white paper. "Oh right, you bastard. Who's been pushing you lot to go along with all his bullshit? You can thank me for this, lads."

"Now all we gotta do is come up with a hit," said George, his usual pessimistic self.

"Don't worry about that," McCartney replied. "We'll do alright. I know we will. But first things first. Anyone for a drink?"

Upon their return from Hamburg seven weeks later, the boys immediately began to ready themselves for their London trip, whittling down to a fine point their already razor-sharp musical instincts during a private, closed-door practice session at the Cavern the first week of June. Several days later, Brian and the boys arrived at EMI House, Manchester Square, London, to sign their contract. Though strictly provisional, if the sessions turned out well and the music and material measured up, the Beatles had themselves a deal. Forty-eight hours later they were bounding up the stone steps of 3 Abbey Road, St. John's Wood, to meet producer George Martin and begin work on what would eventually become their very first single, *Love Me Do*, backed by the romantic ballad, *P.S. I Love You*.

Having made the difficult decision to commence litigation against his three former colleagues in an effort formally to dissolve the group, McCartney was faced with an extended and complicated legal battle. He is seen here with Linda, leaving a London court in 1970.

Paul

Say what you like about Paul and Linda; for the last two-decades-plus they've shared a touching and committed love.

Arriving at the Beatles international corporate headquarters, Apple, housed at 3 Saville Row, just off Piccadilly

Celebrating the birth of Wings at a party held at London's Empire Ballroom, November 8, 1971

Playing daddy to Linda Eastman's little girl, Heather See, while en route to visit Paul's dad, 1969

A rare quiet moment in a very public life

Opposite: **Wings play an impromptu gig at London's Hard Rock Café, March 18, 1973.**

The whole Parlophone experience was a significant high point in the Beatles' ever-advancing assault on the music-loving youth of the world, but behind the scenes there was big trouble brewing. Pete Best, long regarded as the group's handsomest and sexiest member, was soon to experience an excruciatingly cruel twist of fate. After four years of virtually full-time, mind-bending commitment and hard work, the quiet, gentlemanly drummer was about to be cheated out of his one and only shot at the big time.

Following *Please Please Me, From Me to You*, scored big for the Beatles, giving them yet another number-one tune on April 26, 1963. Their next musical coup, the hard-driving, boy/girl mantra *She Loves You*, rocketed to the top of the Melody Maker singles chart on September 7, 1963. Written by Lennon and McCartney in the music room of Jane Asher's parents' house in London, the wild success of *She Loves You* proved once and for all that the Beatles had real staying power as artists. After all, three successive top-flight number-one singles could hardly be called a fluke. Perhaps McCartney's biggest personal thrill of that incredible, eventful year was the Beatles' October 13 appearance on what was then Britain's top television show, *Sunday Night at the London Palladium*.

It was not until the Beatles' heralded appearance at the Royal Variety Performance on November 4 that much news about the charismatic new teen group taking England by storm finally filtered across the sea to America. It was a great honor, to be sure. Jim McCartney was reportedly almost in tears that his son was about to perform before the Royal Family. "Wouldn't Mary be proud," he wondered aloud to his sister Jin, the morning of the grand event. "She is, Jim, she is," came the reply.

At the end of November their fifth single, *I Want to Hold Your Hand*, was released in England and shot directly to number one. A few days later, the group's second LP, *With the Beatles* also came out, amassing immediate advance orders of 2.5 million. Not even Elvis had ever been able to do that.

By the winter of 1964, America was more than ready for the Beatles. Midway over the Atlantic on board Pan Am flight 101 to New York, Paul McCartney was untypically somewhat apprehensive about the reception they might receive. "America has always had everything," he confided to record producer Phil Spector. "Why should we be over there making money? They've got their own groups. What are we going to give them that they don't already have?"

Any lingering doubts were magically swept away when at 1.35 on the afternoon of February 7, 1964, they touched down on Kennedy Airport's long, icy runway. As the plane inched its way to the terminal, the shrill sound of over ten thousand teenage voices, all chanting and screaming for the Beatles, penetrated the hull of the aircraft like gunfire. Peering out of the frosted windows of the DC-10, the Beatles saw for the first time the wild reception America had in store for them. McCartney, for one, was almost in a state of shock.

CHAPTER FOUR

A PRINCE AMONG MEN/PRIDE, PRIVILEGE AND DESPERATION

The latter half of the Sixties saw McCartney increasingly concerned with the pursuit of serious art. Although John Lennon has the reputation of being the "artistic" member of the group, it should be noted that the inspiration and planning for the albums *Sgt. Pepper's Lonely Hearts Club Band*, *Magical Mystery Tour*, much of *The White Album*, and the operatic side two of *Abbey Road* belong almost solely to McCartney.

Long after John, George, and Ringo had retreated to the staid placidity of London's pastoral suburbs, McCartney was burning the midnight oil with the likes of junkie author William Burroughs, beat poet Allen Ginsberg, heralded LSD manufacturer Michael Hollingshead, *International Times* founder Barry Miles, and Marianne Faithfull's husband, John Dunbar, who owned and operated the celebrated Indica Gallery and bookstore on Southampton Row. Through Dunbar, McCartney began to look at art in a new way. Giving himself up to Dunbar's gentle guidance, he soon became a devotee of avant-garde filmmaker Michelangelo Antonioni and a patron of Greek sculptor Takis and his bizarre collection of magnetic machine art.

For a while, the privacy and freedom afforded the Beatles by their rejection of the road was a balm, a breath of fresh air for the stressed-out quartet. After five frantic years of being together night and day, often for months on end, each of them now had the option of wandering off on his own for a while.

Following the unbridled success of their films *A Hard Day's Night* and *Help!*, the Beatles' music became noticeably more introspective, interesting, and intricate.

As early as *Rubber Soul,* Paul McCartney had asserted his colossal talent for melding strong lyrics with widely appealing melodies, as in songs such as *You Won't See Me, I'm Looking Through You*, and *Wait.* All three tunes seem a kind of oblique invitation to his oft-absent lover,

Left: **Playing *Top of The Pops* with Wings**

Below: **Wings in their first and most accomplished line-up.** *Left to right:* **Denny Seiwell (drums), Linda McCartney (keyboards and backup vocals), Paul McCartney (bass guitar and vocals), Denny Laine (rhythm guitar and vocals), Henry McCullough (lead guitar)**

Main picture: Lennon holds forth at a late night recording session, 1967.
Above: The Fab Four, 1964

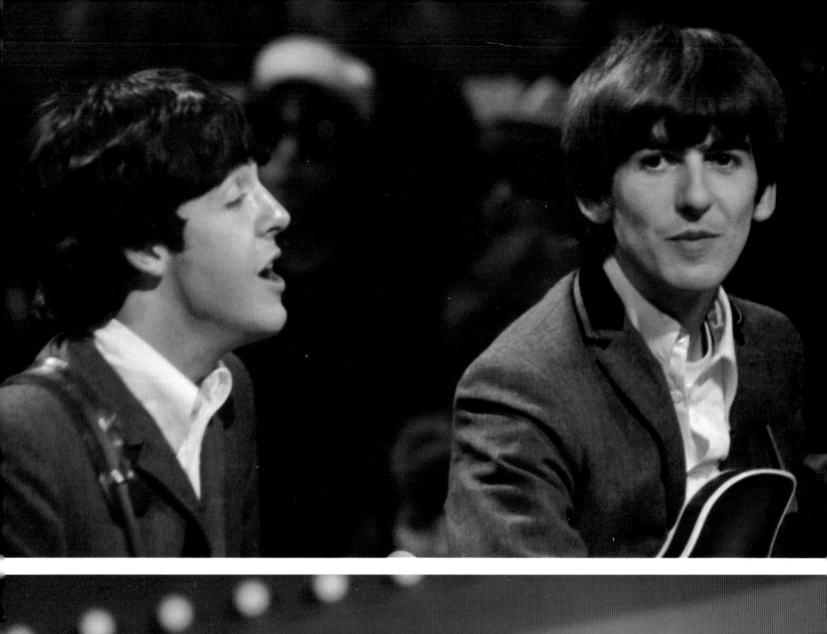

Jane Asher, to anti up emotionally and settle down with him once and for all.

The Beatles' next album, *Revolver*, further showcased McCartney as a musical painter with a wonderfully full and varied palette. Here, for the first time, emerges a truly compassionate Paul, wounded by an uncaring world that capriciously casts aside the broken and lonely, as he portrays in *Eleanor Rigby* and the hauntingly beautiful *For No One*. "At first I thought it (*Eleanor Rigby*) was a bit like *Annabel Lee*, but not so sexy," reflects McCartney.

On Thursday, August 24, just a couple of days prior to Brian Epstein's tragic death from an accidental overdose of sleeping pills, he and the Beatles met to discuss the group's plans for the rest of the year. He is said to have been very keen about Paul's idea for the *Magical Mystery Tour* film and advised his charges to carry on with their plans. Within three days, Brian Epstein was dead. Thrown into a tailspin by this totally unexpected turn of events, the Beatles decided to postpone further work on the film until they returned from a three-month meditation course they had promised to attend at the Maharishi's Rishikesh ashram. A few days later, however, they changed their minds, reasoning that it would make more sense to postpone their holidays until after the filming had been completed.

The idea for *Magical Mystery Tour* first occurred to McCartney while in Denver Colorado with Mal Evans to help celebrate Jane Asher's twenty-first birthday. The concept was simple: the Beatles would invite a select group of close friends, fan club secretaries, bizarre character actors, midgets, and circus freaks to travel around the English countryside with them in a rented coach and just see what happened.

Magical Mystery Tour was first aired on Boxing Day, 1967, on BBC. The *Daily Mail* called it "blatant rubbish," while the *Los Angeles Times* report, "Critics and Viewers Boo: Beatles Produce First Flop with Yule Film." Paul McCartney commented that if the film had been shown in colour as originally intended, rather than black and white, it might have made more sense.

The White Album signalled the beginning of the end for the Beatles as a group. Although they were still working together, they were beginning to grow apart.

The inevitable death knell had already been sounded; the band played on, unwilling troubadours at their own musical wake. "They attempted to be nice to each other when they were laying down the basic tracks," remembers Ken Scott, one of their engineers from the early days of *A Hard Day's Night* and *Help!*

Included on *The White Album* are three of Paul's outstanding miniatures. Perhaps insubstantial in themselves, they work admirably in the context of the expansive two-record set. The first, *Wild Honey Pie*, was originally just a typical McCartney off-the-cuff ad lib which was later edited down and fitted between *Ob-La-Di, Ob-La-Da* and Lennon's silly

Opposite above: **The Beatles live, 1964**
Opposite below: **John and Yoko doing their thing in the early Seventies**

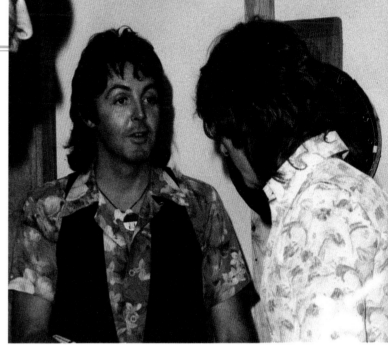

Above left: **Jimmy McCulloch, Wings' bad boy guitarist**

Above right: **Celebrating Denny Laine's birthday**

Right: **Linda and Paul at George Martin's Air Studios on the sunny island of Montserrat**

Bungalow Bill. Of *Wild Honey Pie*, Paul has said, "This was just a fragment of an instrumental which we weren't sure about, but Pattie (Harrison) liked it very much so we decided to leave it on the album.

Although not released until after *Abbey Road*, *Let It Be* was the next full-fledged Beatles project. A fine semi-live album, it also spun off into an intriguing motion picture documentary, and was even made into an excellent picture book.

The sessions for *Abbey Road* began in earnest in July of 1969 with all four Beatles eager to bury the hatchet and get back to making music the way they once did, as a team. At first George Martin was skeptical and only agreed to be coaxed back from his work at his own successful AIR Studios on the condition that the Beatles allow him to direct the sessions as a producer rather than in the relatively subservient fifth-fiddle role he had played on the previous few albums. "*Let It Be* was a miserable experience and I never thought that we would get back together again," Martin recalls.

After assurances from Paul that all would be well, the sessions com-

Opposite: **Paul and Linda decked out for a rare evening out at Mardi Gras in New Orleans**

Opposite inset: **Wings on the road, 1976.**

Below: **Denny, Linda and Paul posing in front of but afew of the countless gold, silver, and platinum records they recieved for their musical accomplishments in Wings**

menced at 2.30 p.m. on July 1, with McCartney overdubbing a lead vocal for *You Never Give Me Your Money*. Arriving well before the others the next day, he laid down the twenty-three-second acoustic track, *Her Majesty*, moving onto *Golden Slumbers* with George and Ringo later in the day.

The next McCartney composition to be recorded was the whimsical *Maxwell's Silver Hammer* on July 9. This turned out to be John's first appearance at this round of sessions; he and Yoko had been waylaid in Scotland after crashing their car into a ditch while visiting with Lennon's Aunt Mater near Durness. Pregnant and under doctor's orders to stay in bed and rest, Yoko was happily accommodated by John who ordered a large double bed be brought into the studio to help facilitate her recovery. Setting up the microphones for the session that morning, the engineers were astounded at this latest Lennon eccentricity. Sometime later, Yoko arrived by ambulance and was carefully lowered onto the mattress by two uniformed attendants. The other three Beatles were not amused. To make matters worse, Lennon insisted a microphone be hung directly over his ailing lover's face in case her highness felt moved to participate! Of course if for some reason John had to pop into one of the other studios for a moment or two for a quick overdub, the bed was simply rolled alongside wherever Lennon happened to perch. All in all vintage Yoko Ono.

On July 17, a lead vocal for another McCartney tune, the brilliant Fifties-inspired *Oh! Darling*, was recorded. This version was ultimately discarded in favour of a stronger, gutsier rendition sometime later.

The End is just that, Paul's final bit of homespun cosmic truth tacked onto the tail of this moving, four-part medley by the Fab Four, perfectly tying together and encapsulating eight years of inspired music from the band the world refuses to forget.

Opposite: **A photo by the author of Paul in Covent Garden**

CHAPTER FIVE

SEPARATE PATHS/HOME AND FAMILY

owards the end of his turbulent Jane Asher days, McCartney visited a clairvoyant in Brighton who told him that he would soon marry a blonde and have four children. By February of 1969 doctors confirmed that his new lady, Linda Eastman, was indeed pregnant. This convinced McCartney that he should cease playing house and make Linda his wife. To his utter amazement, the headstrong Ms. Eastman at first declined.

McCartney kept on pitching, and on March 11, 1969, the Apple press office announced the forthcoming nuptials.

Eight days after the McCartney/Eastman wedding, John and Yoko followed suit and were married on the British-held island of Gibraltar. It was the first time in Paul's recent memory that he had actually managed to pull something off before his old mate got the drop on him, and it felt great.

Mary McCartney, Paul and Linda's first child together, was born at 1.30 a.m. on Thursday, August 29, 1969, at the Avenue Clinic in St. John's Wood. Weighing six pounds, eight ounces, the beautiful baby quickly became daddy's little girl with her proud papa showing her off to the world on the cover of his now-classic *McCartney* album.

By the summer of 1970 it seemed inevitable that the Beatles as a group were almost certainly finished. In June, Lee Eastman (who, along with his son John, now handled McCartney's business affairs) wrote to Allen Klein (John, George, and Ringo's manager) politely requesting that the Beatles' partnership be immediately dissolved.

Hoping that the group could somehow settle their difference amicably and carry on making music, and millions, Klein tried to sidestep

Above: **Onstage during the high-stepping Flowers in the Dirt tour, 1990**

Opposite: **Playing *Top of The Pops* with Wings**

any confrontation with Eastman by simply ignoring his letter. McCartney, however, was by this time adamant, and dashed off a terse note to John suggesting that the Beatles break up once and for all. Several days later, McCartney received a postcard from Lennon reading simply, "Get well soon."

Paul McCartney formally filed suit on Thursday, December 31, 1970, his stepdaughter, Heather's seventh birthday, petitioning the London

Above: **A late night session.**

Above left: **Taking five for a steaming cuppa.**

Opposite: **Wings commander McCartney onstage in a look reminiscent of his *Sgt. Pepper* days**

Opposite: **Together in LA, 1977**

Right: **Playing** *Top of The Pops* **with Wings.**

Below: **Wings take their final bows**

High Court to order the Beatles' partnership dissolved and demand an accounting of all partnership assets and liabilities. John, George, and Ringo were not in any way amused and sought to block the move legally by retaining their own counsel for the long, unpleasant road ahead.

The next big eruption came, predictably, following Paul's first-round victory with the appointment of an official receiver to monitor the group's ever-flowing millions. Henceforth, all the Beatles were forced to cut back their expenditures at least temporarily, in an effort to maintain not only their rapidly rotting Apple empire, but also their own lavish lifestyles.

On the afternoon of the court's appointing a receiver, John, George, and Ringo were together in Lennon's sparkling white Rolls when the bespectacled Beatle got an idea. "Excuse me, Anthony," he said to his chauffeur. "Take us round to Paul's would you. I've got a little going-away present for the cunt." Arriving at the smart address some thirty minutes later, Lennon bounded out of the car and in a single agile leap pulled himself over the famous wall. Seconds later, the latch clinked from the inside. Grinning from ear to ear, Lennon peeped his head out to the others. Walking silently around the classic Phantom Five, he

The McCartneys' Georgian home in St John's Wood

opened the trunk and produced two perfectly new bricks which he then carried the few steps back inside Paul's entrance way. By this time, George and Ringo had stepped out of the car and were standing in the street, their eyes now carefully following John's every move.

Without a moment's hesitation, Lennon drew back his arm and flung one of the bricks through a downstairs window. Almost before the din had subsided he fired off another, smashing an adjacent pane. Flinging open the front door, McCartney stopped dead in his tracks as soon as he saw the culprits. All at once George burst out laughing hysterically, followed by Ringo and John. Seconds later, the three superstar vandals were motoring joyfully down the street, leaving poor McCartney alone on his front stoop, frozen with anger.

The disintegration of the Beatles as a band was hardest on Paul. So very much of everything he does is directed at being accepted and loved and it hurt a lot when his three closest mates began to outgrow the circumscribed world of Beatlehood. From almost day one the Beatles had meant everything to him. Although John started the group, as time went by he gradually relinquished the reins of power to Paul who has hung on mightily ever since. For McCartney the preservation of the Beatles' music, mystique, and lore is a life's work.

Above: **The imposing armored gates to McCartney's London hideaway**

Below: **Their plush dining room at the back of the house**

CHAPTER SIX

BROKEN WINGS/FLYING SOLO

The fall of 1973 saw the final reunion of the Beatles when John, Paul, and George joined forces to help their old pal Ringo boost his then dismal solo career by contributing to what would later become his popular Ringo album. Paul's offering, the syrupy love-gone-wrong tune *Six O'Clock*, worked well within the narrow parameters of Starr's vocal range, as did Lennon's *I'm the Greatest* and Harrison's three - *Sunshine Life for Me*, *You and Me (Babe)*, and the hit single, *Photograph*.

After the Beatles had finally called it quits, Paul and Linda decided to get right back in the saddle and form a new group.

Wings was definitely Paul McCartney's band. Whatever Paul wanted, he got. The feelings and opinions of those around him were largely incidental, especially when it came to allowing his band mates to express themselves creatively. Always image-conscious, McCartney at least tried to appear interested in his colleagues' thoughts and feelings. But it was all a sham; he would simply wait for the others to stop talking and then do exactly as he pleased.

In June of 1974 McCartney decided to replace Wings' first casualty Henry McCullough on guitar. Of several possibilities contemplated, he finally settled on young Jimmy McCulloch, a feisty, hard-drinking Scot from Glasgow, born June 4, 1953.

While in the U.S., apparently, the creative juices began to flow, with the band laying down not only the classic *Junior's Farm*, but also the obscure Jim McCartney instrumental, *Walking in the Park with Eloise*. Later released under the Wings alias, the Country Hams, it is now perhaps the rarest of all McCartney-related cuts. In addition, *Country Dreamer*, the little-known B-side of *Helen Wheels*, was recorded, along with the twangy *Sally G* and several other unreleased country stan-

Left: **Relaxing in the dressing room after the gig**

Below: **Picking up yet another prestigious award**

Above: **At home in Sussex, indulging in one of the McCartneys' favourite pastimes**

Opposite: **Denny and Paul hamming it up for the camera**

dards which involved a number of well-known artists such as Chet Atkins and Floyd Cramer.

Following their month-long stint in Tennessee, the band flew home, where apart from a November 20 appearance on Britain's *Top of the Pops* to promote *Junior's Farm*, nothing of much significance occurred until their January 15, 1975 departure for New Orleans to record tracks for the *Venus and Mars* album. In spite of the gaiety of Mardi Gras and the excitement of working in such a creatively stimulating atmosphere, all was not well among McCartney's musical cohorts.

While it's true that tensions among Wings' inner circle were at an all-time high during this period, the public had no idea of just how deep the wounds were.

The situation had reached the point of no return. Geoff Britton's position in Wings was formally terminated by the McCartneys, who came into his room one morning during the sessions for *Venus and Mars* and casually broke the news.

Once again, smack dab in the middle of an important project without a proper drummer, McCartney was forced to look for a replacement. It was Tony Dorsey, leader of Wings' occasional horn section, who first suggested burly-bearded American, Joe English for the job. Born in Rochester, New York, on February 7, 1949, Joe was eighteen when he joined a local band, Jam Factory. Touring the country for the next six years, English and his fellow Factory workers became well known

as a first-class support group, regularly opening for such pop luminaries as Jimi Hendrix, the Grateful Dead, and Janis Joplin.

Fortunately, *Venus and Mars* was a certified smash. Soaring almost immediately to number one in Britain and America, the clever, well-crafted, impressively packaged album contained such memorable, listenable tunes as *Listen to What the Man Said*, *Letting Go*, and *Rock Show* as well as Denny's stirring *Spirits of Ancient Egypt* and, ironically, the Jimmy McCulloch anti-drug opus *Medicine Jar*.

Altogether, three singles were culled from the album throughout the year, racking up further incredible royalties for the "just plain folks" McCartneys. Some of the Wings natives, however, were growing restless. According to an undated MPL memo titled "Fees for Artists' Services" obtained in the research of this work, Paul's right-hand man, Denny Laine, while reasonably well paid for his creative input, took home nothing close to the millions of pounds his celebrated employer was steadily making off the band.

By 1975, Laine was apparently doing a bit better, taking in a cool $100,000 for his work on *Venus and Mars* and the singles *Listen to What the Man Said*, *Letting Go*, and *Rock Show*.

That summer (1975) Wings rehearsed like demons in a derelict movie house in the nearby town of Rye for what Paul envisioned as a worldwide "tour to end all tours."

Opposite: **Paul outside his office in Soho, 1987**

Posing with The Campbletown Pipe Band, gathered together for the promotional film for the mega-hit *Mull of Kintyre*

Definitely the most photogenic incarnation of Wings, the final, Steve Holly / Laurence Juber, configuration

McCartney playing the fool at Lympne Castle o[n] a break from the rigors of recording

The band decided to test the waters by going out first at home, playing eleven dates between September 9 and September 23. The meticulously orchestrated concerts were well received, bolstering everyone's enthusiasm for the tour ahead.

On October 28, 1975, Wings jetted via Qantas Airlines to Australia. Altogether they did nine shows, commencing at the Entertainment Centre in Perth on November 1. From there they rumbled on to play two shows in Adelaide, two in Sydney, two in Brisbane, and a final two in Melbourne. McCartney remembers this, Wings' first major international outing, "We had fab fun ... The audiences were great and we just dug playing. It was more like a holiday."

So wildly successful were the concerts that tickets were being scalped on the underground for upward of $500, or, what McCartney playfully called, "Sinatra prices."

Making their way back to England, Paul and the band booked themselves into Abbey Road in January of 1976 to begin work on their next album, later called *Wings at the Speed of Sound*. "The idea of that LP," says Denny, "was to try and showcase each member of the band."

Speed of Sound remains a tribute to Paul McCartney's wish to accord his musical cohorts at least a smattering of recognition as individual artists with their own creative agendas.

Issued in May 1976, the album did well, eventually spawning two popular singles, *Silly Love Songs* backed by *Cook of the House* that

Paul, Linda and Denny enjoying the high life

April, and *Let 'em In* sporting the sassy Motown-inspired, *Beware My Love* on the B side, released in July.

The famous Wings Over America tour was scheduled to have begun at the end of March 1976, but had to be postponed due to Jimmy McCulloch's fracture of his index finger during a bar-room brawl in Paris. About a month later the tour kicked off with a show at the Tarrant County Convention Center in Fort Worth.

By June 24, 1976, Wings Over America was history. The night before, at the Forum in L.A., Ringo Starr had walked on stage during the group's final encore and presented his old band mate with a bouquet of flowers. It was a touching scene that seemed to suggest, at least as far as Ringo and Paul were concerned, that the bitter feud over the Beatles' legacy was finally over. At least on a personal level.

Altogether Wings played twenty cities during the six-week tour, reaching over three million rabid fans who often queued for hours to win the chance of seeing the one-time Beatle go through the paces with his new band. While extravagant multi-million-dollar tours are now the order of the day, Wings Over America was the first big show to utilize not only lasers and truck loads of other space-age equipment,

Performing *Hey Jude* live in London, 1968

but also computers and the expertise to pull it all off.

London Town turned out to be quite a fine album. Even Denny was pleased, as he was given the chance to include two solo compositions. "I thought that was a really good record," Laine recalls.

Like *Band on the Run*, *London Town* was more a joint effort by Paul and Denny than the collective effort of Wings. Linda's creative input was minimal, while Joe English and Jimmy McCulloch acted essentially as session men. Among the tunes worked on in earnest by McCartney and Laine were the title track itself, *Morse Moose and the Grey Goose*, *Famous Groupies*, and the ethereal number *Don't Let It Bring You Down*.

Following Wings' extended day in the sun, the band moved on to AIR Studios in London where they continued working through the first half of December. In January 1978 they returned to Abbey Road, polishing off the last bits of the album by January 23.

Now that *London Town* was safely in the can, the group lay back for a bit to plot their next move. Everyone, that is, except Jimmy McCulloch who had left the band on September 8 of the preceding year after a row with his Beatle boss on the farm in Scotland.

The lads take a rare back seat to Ringo while taping an appearance for a 1965 television special.

CHAPTER SEVEN

AFTERMATH/McCARTNEY UNDONE

O n September 12, 1977, Paul McCartney was at last granted his long-held, secret wish for a son when James Louis McCartney was delivered by Cesarian at a London nursing home, weighing in at six pounds, one ounce. Eight days after the birth, the proud parents released an "official" photograph of this, the first male issue from Rock's royal family. "I'm over the moon!" Paul told the evening papers. "When I knew the baby was a boy I really flipped. I was waiting outside the door while he was being born. He has fair hair and looks like Linda. She's still a bit tired, but otherwise smashing. I don't know how she does it."

On June 29, 1978, work began on *Back to the Egg*, Wings' last all-new studio LP. Laying down the basic tracks at Paul's Spirit of Ranachan Studios on the farm in Scotland, new members Steve Holly and Laurence Juber, proved a valuable addition to the band, fitting in well with the gilt-edge poppiness of Denny, Linda, and Paul.

Working like devils on the new album, Wings pulled out all the stops in the hope that *Back to the Egg* might just be the vehicle to toughen up their cream-puff image with a legion of rock watchers weaned on so-called heavyweight acts such as Pink Floyd and the Who. It was not to be. Fragmented, over-ambitious, and sporadic, *Back to the Egg* shipped out to record stores like gangbusters and limped back a couple of months later, a fifty-cent record in a two-dollar sleeve, its failure heralding the end for the band.

One of the happier events of 1979 for Wings was the successful release of McCartney's first decidedly disco single, *Goodnight Tonight*. Issued in Britain on March 23, 1979, the catchy tune did well, reaching as high as number six at home and five in the U.S. What made the pro-

Opposite: **Blackbird**

Following pages: **The grand finale of Magical Mystery Tour**

Right: **Negotiating a particularly narrow thoroughfare.**

ject special, however, had less to do with the music than the spectacular, spare-no-expense video which was produced to promote the release on Tuesday, April 3, at the meticulously preserved Hammersmith Palais Ballroom in London. Produced by MPL and directed by Keef McMillan of Keef & Co., the concept was deceptively simple. The band dressed up in elegant, 1920s-style evening clothes as Paul demonstrated his best Rudy Valee impersonation, crooning into an imposing antique radio mike.

By the late Seventies there was generally a lot of loose talk floating about concerning a potential Beatles reunion. Responding to a nonstop barrage of questions from the prying media, the ex-Beatles often made matters worse by cryptically saying "no" in such a way as to imply the opposite. Of course, the Beatles themselves had not made any final decisions concerning the idea. Paul, especially, would have loved to see his old band back together, if only for one rousing night of music tucked away in the privacy of an obscure rehearsal hall or studio somewhere. John, too, was basically game, often confiding to friends that he found the possibility intriguing.

A lot of people gradually became convinced that if the cause were important enough, or the money right, a reunion just might happen. One such person was Kurt Waldheim (long before his nagging Nazi troubles), at the time Secretary General of the United Nations, who drafted a conciliatory letter to each of the four, asking them to consider getting back together for a concert in aid of the starving masses in war-torn Kampuchea.

McCartney's response was equally diplomatic: he nixed the Beatle idea, offering instead a benefit concert by Wings. So it was that on the evenings of December 26, 27, 28 and 29, 1979, London's Hammersmith Odeon became the site of the Concerts for the People of Kampuchea, McCartney's most overtly humanitarian venture to

Opposite: **Late arrival**

date. Expanded to include other acts such as the Pretenders, Elvis Costello and the Attractions, Queen, Robert Plant, Rockpile, the Who, the Clash, the Specials, Matumbi, Ian Dury and the Blockheads, and, of course, Wings, the series of manic shows ended with the everevolving Rockestra performing three numbers, *Lucille*, *Let It Be*, and the spectacular *Rockestra Theme*.

By January 12, 1980, Paul McCartney felt on top of the world. Springing back mentally after the relative failure of both *Back to the Egg* and Wings' recent British tour, he was ready to take on the world, flying to New York aboard the Concorde on his way to a long-awaited engagement in Japan. After a brief, four-day visit with Linda's dad and an aborted attempt to see John Lennon, the McCartneys checked out of their luxury suite at the Stanhope Hotel and boarded a TWA jumbo jet bound for Tokyo's Narita International Airport.

On the flight over, all McCartney could think about was how the maneuvering, vindictive Yoko had snubbed his efforts to make contact with his former partner.

"This isn't really a very good time," she cooed condescendingly into the telephone, seemingly thrilled to be the bearer of such inhospitable tidings. "We're very busy these days, you know. Maybe next time, okay?"

Landing in Tokyo fourteen exhausting hours later, Paul and Linda emerged from the aircraft all smiles, thrilled to finally be playing Japan. Inside the customs hall they were greeted by a hail of flashing cameras all zeroed in on the great man lugging little James in one arm as he mugged predictably for the delighted media. As they stepped up to the long, low inspection counter, a customs officer indicated to the couple to open their carry-on luggage. "Sure," replied McCartney, revealing no perceivable emotion. Linda, on the other hand, suddenly seemed panicky, her eyes darting back and forth between the small

A Beatle bit-o-memorabilia

rumpled bag and her unsuspecting husband.

Sitting inside what has been widely reported as Linda's overnight case was a small, fist-sized plastic bag obviously containing several ounces of primo pot.

"When the fellow pulled it out of the suitcase," said Paul, "he looked more embarrassed than me. I think he just wanted to put it back in and forget the whole thing, you know, but there it was." A senior officer pushed his way out from behind and immediately ordered the pop star detained. He then radioed for the Narcotics Control Bureau to come and get their man.

"It's all a mistake," Paul said feebly as the Tokyo vice boys slapped on the cuffs and began leading him away. "A serious mistake." To the morally conservative Japanese, McCartney's transgression was indeed a serious matter.

On the ninth day of Paul's incarceration, the powers that be decided he "had been punished enough" and so cut a deal with McCartney's legal staff to release the rock star. Ever the politician, Paul insisted on touring the facility and personally greeting each of the prisoners, which he did, passing his hand through the small iron doors of their cells just to say "Sayonara."

Carted off to the airport, handcuffed, directly from jail, McCartney, surrounded by twelve burly guards, was reunited with Linda and the kids amid dozens of frenzied photographers and reporters clawing at the waylaid Beatle and his family. "Japanese fans are so great," Paul exclaimed to those present in the special VIP departures lounge. "I want to come back again if I'm allowed.

The first musical release following Paul's Japanese sojourn was the somewhat aimless and uneven *McCartney II*. As a strictly solo effort it was competent enough, but somehow never really managed to leave the ground. Issued in Britain on May 16, 1980, it aroused sufficient

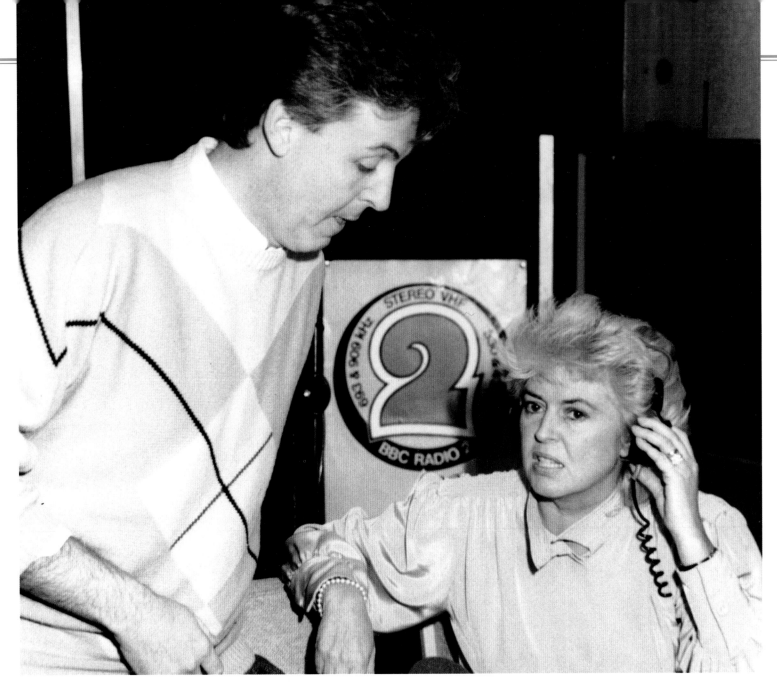

Opposite: **With BBC Radio personality, Gloria Hunniford**

public curiosity as the great one's first post-prison release to propel it all the way to number one. In the U.S., apparently, folks weren't quite as inquisitive, sending the admittedly beautifully packaged gate-fold album to a very respectable number three.

After the roller coaster breakup of the Beatles in 1970 the relationship between John Lennon and Paul McCartney was never really the same. They talked, they met, they still occasionally hung out together, but something had definitely changed. For years people have tried to pin at least part of the blame on their wives, but to do so ignores the complicated, tightly wound interactions between the two. When they fought, they fought like brothers, still maintaining a delicate web of care and concern amid the bitter recriminations of two screaming egos caught in a tug of war for pre-eminence.

Despite Paul's "just kiddin" philosophy, however, for a while there things did get pretty rough. After all the childish name calling back and forth on record and in the media, one of the most personally hurtful episodes to Paul was the time he and Linda turned up unannounced to see John in New York, only to be royally snubbed by his

Previous pages: **Another day another million dollars**

old pal. "Do you mind calling before you come round from now on," Lennon chided. "This isn't Liverpool, ya' know. In New York, you don't just drop in on people like this without warning."

"Sorry, man," McCartney intoned meekly. "We only wanted to stop by for a bit and say hello."

"Yeah, I know, man, but see, I've had a fuckin' long day today with Sean. It's bloody hard work lookin' after a kid this age, you know."

"Well, so ... we'll shove off then. See ya."

The two long-standing friends would never see each other again.

The great abiding problem, of course, still had to do with money. With much of the Beatle millions still largely up for grabs the stakes were high. So high in fact that Lennon went berserk at the mere mention of anything remotely concerned with the group's long-standing financial maelstrom. "At the very end we suddenly realized that all we had to do was not mention Apple if we phoned each other," says Paul. "We could talk about the kids, talk about his cats, talk about writing songs; the one paramount thing was not to mention Apple ... I remember once he said to me, 'Do they play me against you like they play you against me?' Because there were always people in the background pitting us against each other. And I said 'Yeah, they do. They sure do!'"

For all the apparently unrepented rancor that passed between them over the years, when John was killed Paul was reportedly devastated: "He was always a very warm guy, John. His bluff was all on the surface. He used to take his glasses down – those granny glasses – take 'em down and say, 'It's only me.' They were like a wall, you know? A shield. Those are the moments I treasure."

When at last the curtain finally came down on Wings, Paul McCartney felt both vindicated and relieved: vindicated because he had indeed proved to the world that there was life after the Beatles, and relieved that he could now truly strike out on his own without a prop band.

Upon its release *Tug of War* did extremely well. *Rolling Stone*, long impatient with Paul's often uneven post-Beatles work, titled it "McCartney's Gem" and went on to give it their coveted five-star rating. Thought by many to be McCartney's *Imagine*, *Tug of War* neatly strung together the talents of not only George Martin and Denny Laine, but also drummers Steve Gadd and Ringo Starr, guitarist Eric Stewart, bassman Stanley Clarke, as well as guest artists Stevie Wonder and country gentleman Carl Perkins.

Eloquent, sincere, and humble, *Tug of War* (including the LP's spiritually oriented title track) mirrors an inner depth and clarity of vision decidedly lacking in many of Paul's other solo recordings.

Paul's second post-Wings musical adventure (after *Tug of War*) was the flaccid and unfulfilling *Pipes of Peace* released in Britain on October 31, 1983. A haphazard collection of eleven painfully trite and uninteresting compositions, it couldn't be salvaged even by such superstar contributors as Ringo Starr, Andy McKay, Stanley Clarke, Steve Gadd, and the androgynous Michael Jackson. Both Laurence

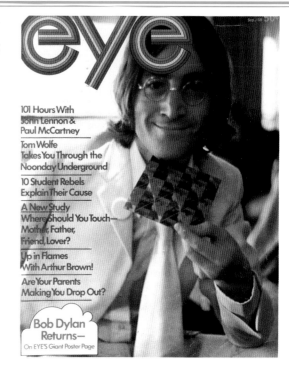

101 Hours With
John Lennon &
Paul McCartney

Tom Wolfe
Takes You Through the
Noonday Underground

10 Student Rebels
Explain Their Cause

A New Study
Where Should You Touch—
Mother, Father,
Friend, Lover?

Up in Flames
With Arthur Brown!

Are Your Parents
Making You Drop Out?

Bob Dylan
Returns—
On EYE'S Giant Poster Page

The September 1968 cover of Helen Gurley Brown's ill-fated underground magazine, Eye

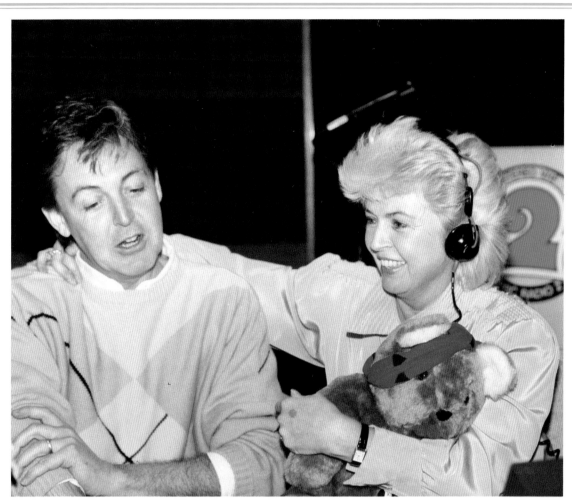

More fun with Gloria Hunniford and Des O'Connor

Rehearsing for the *Magical Mystery Tour*.

Juber and Steve Holly recall rehearsing much of the material included on the album during the final days of Wings, giving credence to the suggestion that the record was basically a throwaway mix of left-overs McCartney had lying around.

Masterfully produced by George Martin, perhaps the biggest break for the album came when Michael Jackson (then impossibly popular) rang up McCartney out of the blue and asked if they might consider working together. "He just said, 'I wanna make some hits,'" remembers Paul. "I said, 'Sounds good.' So he came over. We sat around upstairs on the top floor of our office in London and I just grabbed a guitar and *Say Say Say* came out of it. He helped with a lot of the words on that actually. It's not a very wordy song, but it was good fun working with him because he's enthusiastic. But again, it's nothing like working with John." Another McCartney/Jackson collaboration, *The Man*, was just plain silly, sounding more like the theme song to the *Care Bears* than anything resembling a proper piece of music.

By the early summer of 1986 McCartney was once again itchy to get back up stage before a live audience, a pastime always particularly close to his heart. Issued an invitation to appear at the Prince's Trust Birthday Party at Wembley Arena on June 20, Macca graciously accepted, performing alongside Tina Turner (in a wild rendition of *Get Back*) as well as in a grand slam superstar jam of *I Saw Her Standing There* and the inevitable *Long Tall Sally*. Featuring such regal rockers as Eric Clapton, Elton John, Phil Collins, Mark Knopfler, Howard Jones, Bryan Adams, Ray Cooper, and Midge Ure, the show was a great success. It was first transmitted over the BBC a week later. "The audience was great, it was an incredible back-up band, and I enjoyed every minute," McCartney later remarked.

Paul's next album release, *Press to Play*, was a definite departure for the singer, in many ways more like a far-out Pink Floyd LP than the usual bubble McCartney fare. Not exactly a barnburner commercially, artistically it was just unusual and oblique enough to challenge the listener a bit more than his previous few offerings. Well constructed and flawlessly produced by the team of Hugh Padgham and Paul McCartney, the ten-track opus contained the mature fruit of what appeared to be a lot of creatively intensive soul searching by the artist.

Tunes such as the mystically inclined *Good Times Coming/Feel the Sun*, the otherworldly *Talk More Talk*, and the majestic *Only Love Remains* work well alongside such instantly likeable numbers as *Press* and the lyrically surreal *Pretty Little Head*.

Issued in England on September 1, 1986, Press to Play also boasts cameo appearances by a who's who of celebrated rock 'n' roll greats including Pete Townshend, guitar wizard Carlos Alomar, Phil Collins, Eric Stewart, and old standby Ray Cooper, among others.

The recording that first inspired Paul's second great world tour was the only occasionally absorbing *Flowers in the Dirt*. Hyped by McCartney's minions as the best thing since *Band on the Run*, the thirteen-track work offered little of real import, serving up instead much of the same old McCartney musical mumbo jumbo or what one

critic called, "pop for potheads". "I really took more care with the songs than anything," says Paul. "I wanted an album I could go out on tour with, an album people could relate to. I just didn't want some crummy album dogging the tour."

One of the most impressive aspects of Paul and Linda's life these days is their philosophical commitment to ethical vegetarianism. Linda remembers their reasons for kicking the meat habit, "During the course of a Sunday lunch we happened to look out the kitchen window at our young lambs racing happily in the fields. Glancing down at our plates, we suddenly realized we were eating the leg of an animal that had until recently been gambolling in a field itself. We looked at each other and said, 'Wait a minute, we love these sheep – they're such gentle creatures – so why are we eating them?' It was the last time we ever did."

As time passed and the issue of animal protection became even more volatile and imperative, Paul and Linda both significantly stepped up their efforts on behalf of not only edible livestock but research animals as well. At the risk of being called "radical," late in 1990 they even went so far as to record a series of messages on behalf of PETA (People for the Ethical Treatment of Animals) which were played to callers on a special eight-hundred number throughout North America.

The Beatles' *All you need is love philosophy* had finally and forever blossomed in James Paul McCartney,s heart. It had been a long and winding road.

ACKNOWLEDGEMENTS

Senior Editor: Brenda Giuliano

Executive Researcher: Sesa Nichole Giuliano

The authors would like to thank the following people for their kindness and selfless hard work in helping realize this book.

Sriman Jagannatha Dasa Adikari
Sylvia Baily
Dr. Mirza Beg
Deborah Lynn Black
Al Bremer
Deni Bouchard
Stefano Castino
Srimati Vrinda Rani Devi Dasi
Enzo of Valentino's
Tom Gerrard
Robin Scot Giuliano
Sesa, Devin, Avalon and India Giuliano
Tim Hailstone
ISKCON
Suneel Jaitly
Carla Johnson
Sean Kittrick
Marcus Lecky
His Divine Grace B.H. Mangalniloy Goswami Maharaja
Dr. Michael Klapper
Leaf Leavesley
Donald Lehr
Timothy Leary
Andrew Lownie
Mark Studios, Clarence, New York

David Lloyd McIntyre
His Divine Grave A.C. Bhaktivedanta Swami Prabhupada
Steven Rosen
Self Realization Institute of America (SRI)
Skyboot Productions Ltd.
Sean Smith
Wendell and Joan Smith
Paul Slovak
Something Fishy Productions Ltd.
Dave Thompson
Edward Veltman
Robert Wallace
Dr. Ronald Zucker

Endpapers 'Multiple Realities' by Geoffrey Giuliano, 1993.